Alena Friedrich

The Representation of the Working Class in tl
Full Monty

GRIN - Verlag für akademische Texte

Der GRIN Verlag mit Sitz in München und Ravensburg hat sich seit der Gründung im Jahr 1998 auf die Veröffentlichung akademischer Texte spezialisiert.

Die Verlagswebseite http://www.grin.com/ ist für Studenten, Hochschullehrer und andere Akademiker die ideale Plattform, ihre Fachaufsätze und Studien-, Seminar-, Diplom- oder Doktorarbeiten einem breiten Publikum zu präsentieren.

Dokument Nr. V14482 aus dem GRIN Verlagsprogramm

Alena Friedrich

The Representation of the Working Class in the Films Brassed Off and The Full Monty

GRIN Verlag

Bibliografische Information Der Deutschen Bibliothek: Die Deutsche
Bibliothek verzeichnet diese Publikation in der Deutschen Nationalbibliografie; detaillierte bibliografische Daten sind im Internet über http://dnb.ddb.de/ abrufbar.

1. Auflage 2003
Copyright © 2003 GRIN Verlag
http://www.grin.com/
Druck und Bindung: Books on Demand GmbH, Norderstedt Germany
ISBN 978-3-638-64349-8

Universität Leipzig
Institut für Anglistik

Hauptseminar
Screening Britain: British History and Society in Recent Films
Wintersemester 2002/2003

The Representation of the Working Class in the Films *Brassed Off* and *The Full Monty*

Eingereicht am: 05.01.2003

Table of Contents

INTRODUCTION 3

PART I. THE BRITISH WORKING CLASS IN THE COURSE OF THE 20TH CENTURY 6

    1. The "Old" Working Class   6
    2. The "New" Working Class   7
    3. Summary   8

PART II. THE REPRESENTATION OF THE WORKING CLASS IN THE FILMS *BRASSED OFF* AND *THE FULL MONTY* 10

    1. The Characters' Socio-Economic Situation   10
    2. The Social Bonds   14
    3. Working class Pride and Traditionalism   17
    4. The Workers' Male Identity   20
    5. Regional Identity   22

CONCLUSION 24

BIBLIOGRAPHY 26

Introduction

Social class has always been a basic topic of British film-makers. Especially the New Wave films of the 1950s and 1960s represented class, and particularly the working class, as one of their main issues. At a time of increasing consumerism, Americanisation, commercialisation and growing affluence the lower ranks of society feared a demise of their class identity, as they were traditionally associated with a lower socio-economic status (Hill 2000a: 178; Eley 1995: 19). Later, in the 1980s, Margaret Thatcher's politics of de-industrialisation and individualism destroyed not only a huge part of the workers' traditional working places and, thus, of their social basis, but also of their class identity (Eley 1995: 40; Monk 2000: 275). Now the stress of the films' narrative lay on the social effects of mass unemployment and poverty rather than on the consequences of growing working class affluence and *embourgoisement* (Hill 2000a: 178). As the socio-economic effects of Thatcherism were still noticeable in the 1990s, that decade's films' narrative was also centred around unemployment and social disadvantage of the lower classes.

Two of these films which focus on the lives of working class people in the 1990s are *Brassed Off* (Mark Herman, 1996) and *The Full Monty* (Peter Cattaneo, 1997). Both films take unemployment in traditional working class industries and its social and psychic effects on the people involved as their themes. The main focus of these motion pictures is on working class people and their way to manage their lives without work and financial means.

In this respect, it is particularly interesting to analyse the representations of class, and especially of the working class, in these two films. As films always convey certain ideas and images, and, thus, re-presentations of the "real world", it is of particular significance to filter out these recorded images to understand what 'sense of the world' (Cooke 1996: 298-9) the film is making, i.e. how the film-maker interprets and presents the "world outside" to the viewer. According to Richard Dyer (quoted in Cooke 1996: 299), four different aspects of representation can be considered: First, the *concept* of representation, i.e. the sense of the world the film is making, second, the *typicality* of the representations, i.e. the question of what the film considers to be typical in society, third, the *producers* of the representations, i.e.

the question who is responsible for the representations on screen, and fourth, the *recipients* of the representations, i.e. the audience.

This essay, which is going to analyse the representation of class in *Brassed Off* and *The Full Monty*, will particularly focus on the *typicality* of the representations. The question will be, in which ways the films can be seen as "typical" working class motion pictures. In this respect, the stereotyping of the social classes in these two films will particularly be focused on. Stereotypes are based on oversimplified and preconceived ideas of the characteristics of a particular person, situation or group (Oxford English Dictionary 1989, "Stereotype"). With regard to *Brassed Off* and *The Full Monty*, it will be analysed if classes, and particularly the working class, are represented in such an oversimplified way or if the films represent new and innovative images of the social ranks.

According to Eley (1995: 21), the images and stereotypes of the 'traditional working class culture' as they are presented in many films refer back to 'a historically specific formation of the period between the 1880s and the 1940s'. That was the time when the popular image of the working class was formed; according to Eric Hobsbawm (quoted in Eley 1995: 21) it was 'the working class of cup finals, fish-and-chips shops, palais-de-danse, and Labour with a capital *L*', recognisable 'by the physical environment in which they lived, by a style of life and leisure, by a certain class consciousness increasingly expressed in a secular tendency to join unions and to identify with a class party of Labour'. Yet, although the working class underwent several substantial changes in the course of the 20th century, causing an increasing demise of the traditional working class culture and its distinctive characteristics, many film-makers still fell back on these images and stereotypes when producing a film. In this context, it shall be analysed if the makers of *Brassed Off* and *The Full Monty* also used such stereotypes to produce an image of "the good old working class" as it was many decades ago. In order to gain an understanding of these working class stereotypes, the first chapter of this paper will deal with the "old" working class as it existed at the turn of the 20th century and its main characteristics.

Yet, it shall also be investigated whether *Brassed Off* and *The Full Monty* offer new approaches to the question of class representation, and especially the representation of the working class. Because, as one could expect, not only the traditional working class culture changed drastically during the 20th century, but also

its images and stereotypes as presented in films. According to Hayward (1996: 348), 'stereotypes come and go; they also change in the light of the shifting political cultural context'. That is why it will be examined if this 'shifting political cultural context' found expression in the representation of class in *Brassed Off* and *The Full Monty*. For a better understanding, the characteristics of the "new" working class as it existed at the end of the 20th century will be dealt with in the second chapter.

Part I. The British Working Class in the Course of the 20th Century

1. The "Old" Working Class

The characteristics of the "old" or "traditional" working class are best described by David Lockwood and his colleagues (1966, quoted in Saunders 1990: 108), who had carried out the famous 'Affluent worker' study in 1966 to analyse the British class system. According to him, the "traditional proletarians" consisted mainly of those men who worked in the heavy industries such as coal mining, shipbuilding or in the steel industries. These workers were above all characterised by a very strong sense of community, solidarity and fraternalism. As they mostly worked in small and cohesive groups in which they came to know and rely upon each other, a very strong attachment to one's workmates became a traditional signifier of the working class status. These men did not only work together but they also helped each other as best as they could and fought for their rights in unionised groups. As Cashmore (1989: 13) claims, 'working class people have shown impressive solidarity in defence of what they take to be their interests' throughout history. Yet, the emotional bonds of fraternalism between the workers did not only exist at the workplace, but were often carried over into their personal life outside. Apart from their work in the factories or the pit, the workers also tended to spend their leisure time in pubs and clubs with their workmates. In contrast to that, the attachment of the workers to women seems to have been much weaker, because, as Lockwood (1966, quoted in Saunders 1990: 108) says, 'wives and daughters lead strikingly separate lives based on the home'. Apart from the intense relationship between the workers, only the emotional bonds between father and son seem to have been equally robust as the bonds between the workers.

The strong sense of community and belonging together between the workers led to a powerful sense of class solidarity and pride within the working class which, furthermore, resulted in a noticeable turning away from the ruling classes. As Lockwood (1900, quoted in Saunders 1990. 108) says, a clear class division

between "us", i.e. the workers, and "them", i.e. the bosses helped to form a distinct working class identity.

Yet, the local factory did not only determine the workers' lives but also the life of the whole community. According to Lockwood (quoted in Saunders 1990: 108), entire villages and towns were often grouped around a single source of employment, such as the local pit, shipyard or dock, which also shaped the physical surrounding of the working people.

Apart from the mentioned characteristics of the traditional working class culture – solidarity, community, fraternalism and pride – Stedman and Gareth (1983, quoted in Haywood 1997: 14) name some further 'conspicuous icons' of working class life which are, above all, symptomatic for the proletarians' personal lives: the extended family, the terraced street, the pub, football matches, the sporting paper, the race track, the music hall, the Sunday stroll and the holiday excursion. Additionally, Haywood (1997: 109) names traditional working class cultural activities such as the brass band.

2. The "New" Working class

Since World War II the British class system has been undergoing numerous drastic changes which also influenced the traditional working class life and its typical features.

While poverty played a dominant role in many proletarians' lives during the 19th and the beginning 20th centuries, the working class entered a period of unparalleled prosperity in the 1950s. They profited, above all, from the remarkable economic changes in Britain after the Second World War which resulted in a steady economic growth and, thus, full employment for most workers and a general rise in their living standards. However, this development also led to an increasing anxiety that consumerism and mass culture would erode the workers' class identity and that the affluence would assimilate the working class into an expanding *bourgeois* lifestyle (Haywood 1997: 91-93).

Another drastic change for the working class culture came with the 1980s and Margaret Thatcher's politics. Her policies of monetarism, deregulation and de-industrialisation resulted in a far-reaching reshaping of the working class. Above all, the weakening of the workers' economic basis, namely their industries, led to mass

unemployment and made the term "working" in working class more and more meaningless. Mainly the staple industries, such as shipbuilding, steel and coal, were hit by Thatcher's policies of de-industrialisation. Furthermore, her crushing of trade union power deprived the workers of a huge part of their traditional class identity (Haywood 1997: 139-140; Green 1990: 28; Dorey 1999: 179-181). After several years of affluence and rising living standards, the working class now again experienced social and economic inequalities such as unemployment, low wages, poor housing and education. However, the study *Social Class in Modern Britain*, carried out by Gordon Marshall and his colleagues in 1984, found out that the class consciousness and pride among the workers returned during these hard years as the increasing social and economic inequalities between the lower and higher ranks reawakened the "us" vs. "them" feeling (quoted in Marwick 1990: 366).

Even though Margaret Thatcher was replaced by John Major in 1990, the economic and social conditions of the working class people in Britain remained almost the same. As Dorey (1999: 183) says, 'he [John Major] did nothing to foster a new, closer relationship with the trade unions, nor did he seek to provide workers with greater employment protection or job security'. As Dorey (1999: 196) points out, the time of Major's premiership was characterised by '"down-sizing", "delayering", longer working hours, pay cuts, job insecurity, and "macho management"'.

Nevertheless, it needs to be mentioned that the traditional working class as it had existed in the 19th and 20th centuries was more and more vanishing in the course of the 20th century (Saunders 1990:117; Marwick 1990: 363). Above all, the lack of the workers' economic basis, the growing consumerism and technological advance made employment in the manual heavy industries increasingly unnecessary. As workers in such industries were exclusively male, the loss of work also meant a loss of male and masculine identity. In contrast to that, the expanding service sector led to an increasing presence of women in working life. While they were mainly bound to house and housework in the previous decades, they now more and more participated in public life.

3. Summary

The British working class experienced far-reaching changes in the course of the 20th century. Until the Second World War the working class people and their

lives were still very much associated with work which was exclusively connected with men. There was a noticeable separation between women, working at home and spending their lives mostly in the private space, and men, working in the heavy industries and being part of public life. The men's lives were characterised by a strong sense of fraternalism, solidarity and community and a remarkable class pride.

After World War II, working class people experienced a short-lived affluence and a time of full employment. Yet, in the course of Margaret Thatcher's premiership during the 1980s these traditional hallmarks of the working class culture were increasingly weakened. Above all, the destruction of the heavy industries deprived the workers of their economic and also social basis, and, thus, of their traditional working class identity.

The following film analysis is going to investigate in what way these class issues find expression in *Brassed Off* and *The Full Monty*. It will be looked upon traditional and somewhat stereotypical representations of the working class as well as upon representations of changing features of today's working class.

Part II. The Representation of the Working Class in the Films *Brassed Off* and *The Full Monty*

1. The Characters' Socio-Economic Situation

Both films, *Brassed Off* and *The Full Monty*, have one thing in common: the topic of unemployment. Regarding this, the films' concern with the growing problem of mass unemployment since the 1980s becomes obvious. And even the joblessness of men who had worked in a branch of the heavy industry is depicted in the films: *Brassed Off*, on the one hand, is about miners who just stepped into the process of losing their job, and *The Full Monty*, on the other hand, about steel workers who have already lost their jobs since their factory was closed.

However, as Monk (2000: 278) puts it, the problem of the films is not unemployment per se, but its psychic and emotional effects on the characters. This feature is, above all, represented in *Brassed Off*, as the film shows the workers' way to unemployment and its consequences. At the beginning of the film all men are still employed in the local coal pit. They are happy to work and seem to be optimistic about their future. However, as the following scenes show, this secure future is threatened by an announced closure of the pit. The workers' optimism changes into scepticism and anxiety about the forthcoming developments. Although a ballot among the workers still gives them the chance to decide between a redundancy payment and the final closure of the pit, and a viability study of the pit which might ascertain it as profitable and avert its closure, the majority of the miners has already lost its hope for a secure future and votes for redundancy.

The psychic and social consequences of the forthcoming unemployment hit, above all, Phil, one of the workers. He not only has to fear the loss of his home and his family, but also of his relationship to his father Danny. On the one hand, the approaching joblessness deprives him of the opportunity to improve his financial situation. Before the pit closure Phil and his wife Sandra already have to struggle to survive and feed their family, as Phil still has to pay off his old debts of 12,000 pounds. His family's poverty becomes particularly obvious in a scene where Sandra cannot even pay her supermarket purchases as she lacks 60 pennies. However,

that situation gets even worse after the pit closure. Since Phil is no longer able to pay off his debts, the bailiffs seize his entire property and leave him only with the telephone. Apart from that material loss, the pit closure also threatens his social relationships to his family and his father. First, Sandra leaves him with their four children, as Phil is now no longer able to feed his family. Yet, Sandra's decision to leave her husband also stems from her despair about Phil's attachment to the local colliery band. As it seems that Phil is more interested in the band than in his family and invests money in the band and a new instrument despite the family's financial situation, Sandra does not see any other way out than to leave him (although the viewer does not learn where she goes). However, Phil's devotion to the band is rather a gesture of friendship to his father Danny who leads the colliery band and who tries to hold the band together in those hard days. However, these close bonds between father and son are also threatened by the pit closure, since Phil and the other band members are no longer able to finance the band and, thus, deprive Danny of his only purpose in life. Phil, who occupies kind of a role of mediator between the other workers and Danny, becomes heavily torn between his loyalty to his father and his workmates and his financial situation. This dilemma plus the loss of his family and his home finally drive Phil to suicide. In this respect, Phil's development from a happy worker and band member to a man who has lost everything in life – 'wife, kids, house, job, self-respect, hope' – and who, eventually, attempts suicide depicts the psychic and social consequences of unemployment in a very clear and intense way.

In *The Full Monty* the topic of suicide is also dealt with; however, in a much less subtle way. In one scene Lomper attempts suicide, but actually the viewer does not exactly know why. Lomper's life is not described in the same detailed way as Phil's life is and so the *The Full Monty* leaves it to the viewer's imagination if unemployment and a bad financial situation or maybe something else was the reason for Lomper's suicide attempt.

As a matter of fact, *The Full Monty* is, in general, far less concerned with the topic of unemployment and its effects on the people than *Brassed Off* is. One rather gets the impression that the characters of *The Full Monty*, who have been jobless for a longer time than the workers in *Brassed Off*, have already surrendered and have learned to live with their new life without work. In contrast to the miners of *Brassed Off*, the former steel workers in *The Full Monty* have already lost their hope

and consider their visits to the job centre rather a necessary evil than a chance for a new life.

The social consequences of unemployment in *The Full Monty* are best represented by the relationship between Gaz and his son Nathan. Mandy, Gaz's ex-wife who has been given the custody of Nathan, threatens Gaz to take away his right to see Nathan in case Gaz should not pay his maintenance payment. However, since Gaz receives social security, he has difficulties in paying the maintenance, which, consequently, endangers his relationship to Nathan. Furthermore, Gaz cannot really offer his son a pleasurable life with all the things children wish whenever they see each other. For instance, he can only offer him tickets for a soccer match of a local team, although Nathan wishes to see Manchester United. Gaz even cannot offer Nathan the food he wants: as one scene shows, Nathan has to eat Chinese food although he does not like it, because his father cannot afford the meals Nathan likes. In this respect, the father-son relationship is threatened by Gaz's unemployment and lack of financial means in the same way as Phil's relationship to his father in *Brassed Off* is threatened by the missing possibility to finance the band after the pit closure.

Yet, in general, the social and emotional effects of unemployment are much subtler presented in *Brassed Off* than in *The Full Monty*. This stems, however, to a big part from the fact that *The Full Monty* is supposed to be a comedy and *Brassed Off* rather a tragic comedy. However, as a matter of fact both films do deal with the topic of unemployment and, thus, stray from the traditional representation of the working class men as being employed in a factory. Both films mirror the recent developments within the labour market and, therefore, show a more realistic and less stereotypical picture of the working class as it is nowadays.

Apart from the characters' unemployment in both films, other representations of the characters' socio-economic status (which, however, are mainly caused by the unemployment) can be observed. In *Brassed Off* as well as in *The Full Monty* the working class characters are depicted as people without considerable means. This is, firstly, represented in the characters' concrete lack of money. In *The Full Monty* Gaz has his pockets full of small change, goes shopping at the flea market and at ASDA (a typical British low-price supermarket), and steals cars (or at least talks of it), sweets and a video. When he first wants to buy the video, he and his friends cannot even pay the special price of 4,99 Pounds for it. In *Brassed Off*, apart from

Phil's and his family's financial problems, some of the members of the colliery band cannot pay their share to the band's cash box anymore.

Secondly, the low socio-economic status of the films' characters is represented through their housing. In *The Full Monty* Gaz lives in a council flat which Nathan describes as being 'messy and cold'. Dave, another main character of the film, as well as the workers in *Brassed Off* live in typical terraced houses. Moreover, *Brassed Off* shows the characters' lives in the walled courtyards; how women talk with each other from yard to yard and how a man relaxes on a sun-bed reading the newspaper. In contrast to that, the middle-class characters live in more exclusive accommodation. In *The Full Monty* Gaz's ex-wife Mandy lives together with her new partner in a nice and clean detached house with insulation windows, and Gerald, the workers' former foreman, in a detached house in a 'good area' with gnomes in the front garden. In *Brassed Off* Gloria, who works for the pit's management, moves into a guest-house above the local pub.

A third feature which represents the socio-economic status of the characters is their private property, i.e. clothes, cars, etc. In this respect, clear differences between the classes are noticeable as well. *Brassed Off*'s as well as *The Full Monty*'s characters wear rather leisure and loose clothes such as denims, cotton shirts and jumpers. Gaz, whose only expensive garment seems to be the leather jacket he is wearing all the time, does not even have a suit for a funeral and, thus, has to steal it. Concerning cars, none of the working class characters in *The Full Monty*, apart from Lomper who, however, drives a car ready for the scrap-heap, seems to have a car. In *Brassed Off* Jim drives a Vauxhall, the typical British low-budget car. Since his colleagues do not have a car, Jim gives them a lift in his car every day when they go to or come from work. Danny owns a bicycle and some of the other workers from the pit are also seen how they sadly and pessimistically wheel their bicycle home after the ballot. In contrast to that, the films' middle-class characters can clearly be differentiated from the lower ranks by their property. In *The Full Monty* Mandy and her new partner own an almost new car and wear smart clothes. Gerald and his wife Linda possess a sun-bed and Gerald, even though he has lost his job as a foreman, is still wearing a suit every day. He does that, above all, to give his wife the impression that he is still working, because she does not know that he has lost his job. In *Brassed Off* the middle-class people are equally depicted: Gloria behaves in a fairly elaborate way at the beginning of the film, owns

a laptop and wears chic clothes such as cotton and silk blouses, skirts, mohair pullovers and stilettos. Her boss, furthermore, wears suits and has a car with a chauffeur. The only thing which seems untypical for the middle-class is Gloria's VW Beetle. However, one may assume that the film tries to depict Gloria's sympathy for the pit workers and, thus, for the working class by that.

Considering all the mentioned representations of the working class concerning its socio-economic status, it becomes obvious that, on the one hand, both films include recent developments within the working class by dealing with the topic of unemployment and its psychic and social effects on the people involved. However, *Brassed Off* and *The Full Monty* also fall back upon traditional stereotypes of the working class such as poor housing, lack of money and property, and simple clothing.

2. The Social Bonds

In both films two distinctive social relationships between the characters can be made out: a father-and-son relationship and the relationship between the workmates.

In both films the relationship between father and son is based less on a harmonic and indestructible dependence but rather on a relationship which is about to break down due to various external influences. However, both films represent the bonds between father and son as being so strong that even the worst crisis cannot destroy them. Actually, these bonds become even stronger because of that. In *The Full Monty* the relationship between Gaz and his son Nathan is based upon the problem that Gaz has lost the custody of Nathan and is now trying to spend as much time with him as possible and to be him a good father. Gaz takes Nathan everywhere, even to the Chippendales performance and to Gaz friends' strip training. In contrast to that, Nathan is very rarely seen with his mother though she has the custody of him. Thus, the viewer gains the impression that the problem of Gaz having lost the custody of Nathan is not really existent but is rather used as an alibi for the film's narrative, since Gaz's reason for his and his workmates' strip performance is to earn enough money to be able to pay the maintenance for Nathan so they can still see each other. The relationship between Gaz and his son seems to be very strong. They spend almost all their time together and Nathan stands by his

father even though Gaz treats him wrongly from time to time and Nathan is ashamed of his father stripping at the beginning of the film.

In *Brassed Off*, Phil also tries to stand by his father and, above all, by Danny's affection for the colliery band. In this respect, Phil even risks the breakdown of his family, since he ignores his wife's threat to leave him in case he continues to finance the band. Phil realises that music and the band is everything that matters in his father's life and, thus, cannot tell him that the other members of the band decided to leave the band when the pit is going to be closed and that they also decided not to go to the final brass band competition in the Royal Albert Hall in London. The bonds between Phil and Danny become even stronger when Danny, who suffers from pneumoconiosis, collapses after having heard that the pit workers voted for redundancy, which does not only mean the closure of the pit but also of Danny's band.

As a matter of fact, the external influences which threaten the relationship between father and son seem to be more plausible and better displayed in *Brassed Off* than in *The Full Monty*. While Gaz's loss of the custody of Nathan appears more like a pretext for the narrative and the relationship between them seems not really to be under threat, Phil often seems to doubt his loyalty to his father since he realises that he does not only risk his relationship to his family by that but also to his workmates. However, at the end Phil decides to stand by his father (even though he seems to feel pangs of conscience), which shows his strong attachment to Danny. Despite the different representations of the father-son relationship in *The Full Monty* and *Brassed Off*, the idea that sons need their fathers (Monk 2000: 282) is clearly depicted in both films.

Another feature of the characters' connection to each other is the relationship between the workmates – in *The Full Monty* between the strippers who used to work together in the local steel works, in *Brassed Off* between the coal miners of the local pit. Both films represent the traditional aspects of working class identity very clearly, namely strong attachment to the workmates, solidarity and mutual aid. As a matter of fact, both films' narrative is centred around the male groups and, thus, focus mainly on the relationships between men. In exactly the same way as the father-and-son relationships in the two films are inviolable, the strong bonds between the workmates cannot be threatened by any crisis. According to Monk (2000: 282), the 'healing powers' of male bonds help to stand up to all occurring difficulties. And, as

Hill (2000a: 183) puts it, both films establish a 'certain utopianism about the possibilities of collective action' and lead to a 'recovery of the collective spirit even if the shared experience of work which they originally grew out of has disappeared'.

However, as one may assume, this 'shared experience of work' has merely been replaced by a shared experience of fate. Both films focus on the characters' unemployment and the resulting emotional and social ups and downs the men have to face. However, in contrast to *The Full Monty*, the miners in *Brassed Off* are still linked with each other by their employment in the pit at the beginning of the film. One can see them working together in a team, how they scrub each other's backs in the shower after work and how they go home together. Apart from their work in the pit, the male characters of the film are also bound to each other through the band where they seem to meet several times a week. Furthermore, they spend most of their leisure time together, playing pool and drinking beer in the pub. Even though they lose their work and, thus, also their shared social basis in the course of the film, they stand by each other through the hard times. Despite the financial problems they now have to face and the impending dissolving of the band, they stick together, above all, to do Danny a favour. Moreover, after Danny's collapse they collect money for a present despite their critical financial situation. After Phil's suicide attempt they comfort him and invite him for a beer, hoping that he will forget his sorrows as fast as possible. The miners try to help each other as good as they can, whereby the viewer even gets the impression that they can only be helped by their comrades. Any occurring problem they discuss with their workmates rather than with their wives or any other person.

Yet, in contrast to *Brassed Off*, women have a say in the men's problems in *The Full Monty*, and, as can be seen with regard to Dave, even a stronger one than the male comrades. After having decided to become a member of the stripper group, Dave, who is a bit stocky, starts to be concerned about his body and his outer appearance. His wife and even his male friends cannot relieve him from his lack of self-esteem. Gaz tries several times to convince Dave, who now decided not to take part in the public strip performance, to come back to the group. Yet, finally, only Dave's wife Jean can take away his inferiority complex and convince him to participate in the show.

However, in general, the male bonds in *The Full Monty* are as strong as they are in *Brassed Off*. That intense attachment to the workmates becomes, above all,

obvious at the beginning of the film when Gaz and Dave look out for members for their strip group. Even though they do not know Lomper personally, they make him give up his suicide attempt and offer him to become friends just because they know that he had worked in the same steel factory as they had. Equally, they admit Gerald, their former foreman, as a member of the stripper group, since he had worked with them in the preceding years and now shares the same fate of unemployment.

As this chapter has shown, the social bonds between father and son and between the workmates as they are shown in *Brassed Off* and *The Full Monty* refer very much to the traditional images of the working class. Therefore, these films cannot be placed into Monk's (2000: 280) category of the '1990s underclass film' in which, according to her, the loss of homosocial communities and the powerful emotional bonds associated with them are depicted.

3. Working class Pride and Traditionalism

According to Monk (2000: 275), *Brassed Off* and *The Full Monty* do not only establish a strong sense of collectivity and community, but also a distinct class consciousness. In Hill's (2000a: 183) opinion that 'recovery of pride and self-dignity' in the working class films of the 1990s can be attributed to the economic adversity and social decay in Britain during the 1980s and 1990s under Margaret Thatcher and John Major.

In *The Full Monty* the working class pride is very much represented with regard to the different kinds of occupation the characters are offered at the job centre. As a matter of fact, Gaz and his friends never really seem to look for new jobs, but prefer to spend their time in the job centre playing cards. One gets the impression that they regard their visits to the job centre rather as pastime and a necessary evil than as a chance for a new job. Most of the jobs which are offered to them seem to be beneath them. As they had worked in a formerly respected position at the local steel works which had demanded a great deal of physical power of them, they now still hope to find jobs as steelworkers which are, however, no longer offered due to the altered labour market. Still, they keep their pride and decide rather to be jobless than to work in an inferior position. Dave, who is offered a job as a security guard at a supermarket first refuses it, but later he decides to accept it; however, obviously

only to be able to watch his wife who works at the supermarket and who Dave believes to have an affair with a colleague. Yet, after having worked several days at the supermarket he decides rather to be together with his friends in the strip group than to continue his work in a position which seems to be not adequate for him. In contrast to Gaz and his working class friends, Gerald seems to be the only one who really looks for a new job at the job centre and who, finally, also finds a new occupation. As a matter of fact, he is also very much driven by his class pride. Just as Gaz and his friends are proud of their former occupation at the steel works and of what they have produced there with their own hands, Gerald is proud of his former position as a foreman and all the social and financial conveniences it meant. Being admitted as a new member of the strip group, he first refuses to work in such an inferior and embarrassing position. However, finally he decides to take part in the show, even though he just found a new job in his position. Furthermore, he is so embarrassed of having lost his former job as a foreman that he does not tell his wife about it for six months but pretends to still have the job.

In contrast to *The Full Monty*, the workers in *Brassed Off*, who have just lost their jobs, still hope that they will find a new occupation. It seems that the characters of *The Full Monty*, who obviously have been unemployed for a longer time already, already know the new labour market and know that they will not be offered jobs in the staple industries anymore, and, thus, have resigned. For the characters of *Brassed Off*, however, it seems to be the first time that they are unemployed and that they, therefore, tackle their search for a job more optimistically.

In general, however, the issue of working class pride in *Brassed Off* can best be observed with regard to the colliery band, an important feature of working class identity. The band has already been existing since 1881 and has, according to Danny, survived any crises, i.e. 'two world wars, three disasters, seven strikes [and] one big, bloody depression'. However, Danny's pride for the band is not shared by his band members anymore. Since they fear the closure of the pit, they also fear not to be able to finance the band and, above all, their families anymore. Danny, for whom the band is the only thing that matters in life, struggles hard to hold the band together and, thus, to keep an old working class tradition alive. Hallam (2000: 266) also says that this 'keeping the band together and making sure it continues to play symbolises a rather desperate attempt to maintain the collective dignity of the community and keep its values intact'. The question the miners ask themselves is,

however, if such a tradition is of use if it does not refer to anything anymore, i.e. if it is useful to maintain a colliery band after the pit has been closed. As the majority of the band members says that a colliery band cannot exist without a pit, the tradition of the band and, thus, of an important hallmark of working class life is under serious threat. In Danny's opinion, however, the band has to continue to exist after the closure of the pit, just to maintain one of the last working class traditions and, moreover, the memory of the coal pit. As he says, the band will be the only 'reminder of hundred bloody years of hard craft' after the closure of the pit. Yet, it is a rather hopeless attempt to hold the band together. Secretly, Danny already knows that he has lost the fight and that he cannot convince his musicians not to leave the band. Consequently, he collapses when he learns that the pit is going to be closed. Despite the film's happy ending – that the band goes to London and wins the national competition of brass bands in the Royal Albert Hall – the viewer can picture to himself that this was the last appearance of the band and that not only the local pit but also the band as part of the village's and the workers' identity are gone. Above all, Danny's speech before the audience at the end of the film shows that he also realised that music and the band is not the only thing that matters in life and that the miners' lives are more important than keeping an old tradition alive.

The only thing the characters in *Brassed Off* seem really to be proud of is the Great Miners' Strike of 1984[1] even though the workers lost it. Yet, as it marked the last and probably one of the most imposing workers' rebellions, the characters of *Brassed Off*, who took part in the strike, are still extremely proud of it. For instance, Phil proudly announces that he participated in the strike, and Andy finds it better to be called a 'fucker' than a strike-breaker, referring back to the Great Strike. However, by and large, all that remains of the strike is a memory of it. The miners would have the chance to fight against the closure of their pit once again. Yet, as it seems they have already resigned and do not do it. Harry's wife remembers that he had been 'full of fight' during the Great Strike and criticises that he has now lost all his fighting spirit and accepts his fate. Moreover, Danny remarks in his speech at the end of the film: 'Most of them [the miners] lost the will to win a while ago. I fear they even have lost their will to fight'. In this respect, one realises that not only the tradition of the colliery band is gone but also the workers' pride and will to fight.

---

[1] After the closure of several pits and the destruction of ten thousands of jobs by Margaret Thatcher at the beginning of the 1980s, miners all over Britain joined together to fight against Thatcher's destructive politics (Green 1990: 32,35).

This aspect of lost hope among the workers is apparent in both films. In *The Full Monty* as well as in *Brassed Off* the topic of suicide is dealt with. In *The Full Monty* Gaz, Dave and Lomper even ponder how to commit suicide in the most efficient way. Apart from that, Phil's comment in *Brassed Off* about miners being 'dinosaurs [and] mammoths' mirrors the hopelessness of his life and his work. Even the old working class tradition of "us" versus "them", i.e. the workers versus their bosses or any other superior persons, is no longer stressed. Although the workers in *The Full Monty* denounce Gerald at the beginning of the film ('You're no longer our foreman. You're just like the rest of us. Scrap.'), they later admit him as a member of the strip group. And in *Brassed Off* Andy even sleeps with Gloria, 'the enemy', as he says. As these 'populist alliances' (Hill 2000a: 184) show, the traditional class consciousness of the workers becomes more and more lost, above all, because the shared fate makes class boundaries obsolete.

The overall picture of both films concerning class pride and class consciousness is that time has caught up with the films' working class characters and their traditions. In this respect, *Brassed Off* and *The Full Monty* contradict the traditional working class attributes of class pride and dignity.

4. The Workers' Male Identity

Traditionally, the workers were defined by their work and, thus, by their 'masculine physicality' (Eley 1995: 18). The films of the 1950s were still very much centred around that issue, whereas the films of the 1990s increasingly dealt with the topic of unemployment and, therefore, of a 'weakening of those ideologies of masculinity which have traditionally underpinned both work and trade union actions' (Hill 2000a: 178). Men did now not only lose their 'male working class labour power' but also their 'male gender power' (Monk 2000: 279), meaning the loss of their typical social roles as wage earners and head of the family (Hill 2000a: 178). As Monk (2000: 279) puts it, the closure of the heavy industries was accompanied by the weakening of ideologies of traditional male masculinity. By that, the films of the 1990s dealing with working class issues were very much centred around men and the impact of long-term joblessness, poverty and social exclusion on them.

Undoubtedly, *Brassed Off* and *The Full Monty* can be placed into this branch of films. Above all, the role change between the films' male and female characters

needs to be analysed in more detail. While the presentation of women in the New Wave films of the 1950s was very much confined to domesticity (Eley 1995: 20), the films of the 1990s, and particularly *The Full Monty* and *Brassed Off*, show women taking over men's places as well as men's roles. In *The Full Monty*, for instance, women visit a performance of the Chippendales in a Working Men's Club, a traditional male space in which women are usually only allowed if they are related to a male member and then only in limited circumstance (Monk 2000: 281). Moreover, women are seen in the streets, another traditional male space, and even in the men's toilet. They drink beer, urinate standing up, turn their heads to look at men and whistle after them. Furthermore, women do have jobs in *The Full Monty*, men do not. Dave's wife Jean works at the supermarket and Mandy as a supervisor in a textile factory. Concerning all that, men are no longer represented as the family's wage earner and the main contact to the outside world in *The Full Monty* (Teske 2002: 50). As Gaz remarks in the film, men will not be needed anymore in the near future, they will be 'obsolete, dinosaurs, yesterday's news'.

Yet, in contrast to women taking over male spaces and roles, the male characters of the film now start to take over women's roles and to behave like them. Thinking of their strip performance in front of hundreds of women watching their bodies, Gaz and his friends start to critically look at themselves and to question their outer appearance. They begin to see themselves as they normally see women and become concerned about their weight or the length of their penises. They give each other beauty tips, do sport and use the sun-bed. Dave even refuses his wife to have sex with him, because he considers himself too fat. Apart from that, the fact that the male characters of *The Full Monty* strip is a strong evidence for the role change between men and women.

In *Brassed Off* the role change between male and female characters can be noticed as well. For instance, it is the female characters who strike against the closure of the pit and their husbands' unemployment. By that, the film refers back to the Great Miners Strike when women had already actively taken part in a strike. As Haywood (1997: 189) points out, they broke down traditional notions of the women's place in a very traditional community by that and destroyed the idea that only those whose jobs were threatened could fight a strike. With regard to *Brassed Off*, the striking women in the film clearly represent that idea of breaking down traditional notions of the women's role. Yet, the role change in that film becomes obvious in

many more scenes: For example, Jim's and Ernie's wives call their husbands man without 'bollocks', since they did not have the courage to leave the brass band. Danny asks Phil, who has bruises all over his face after the bailiffs have punched him, whether his wife Sandra has beaten him. Thus, he believes that Sandra is capable of doing something which formerly men were mostly accused of. And, moreover, Gloria is taking over a traditional male place by becoming a member of the colliery band. However, in contrast to the female characters in *The Full Monty* Gloria is not really changing her role, since she is not actively taking over that male space but is let into it. Additionally, Danny admits her as a member of the band only because her grandfather had been a very famous wind player and miner and because she was born in Grimley, the village *Brassed Off* is set in. Thus, the dividing lines between men and women are basically still existent in that case, since probably no other woman who does not have the same "qualifications" as Gloria has would be allowed in the band.

In general, *The Full Monty* focuses much more on the subject of the emancipation and role change of women than *Brassed Off* does. However, one could argue that since *Brassed Off* is set in a small provincial village, old traditions and role models are kept much longer than in a big, modern city such as Sheffield, where *The Full Monty* is set.

Yet, despite the increasing representations of changing gender roles in the two films, and, above all, in *The Full Monty*, some "typical" issues of the male gender role can still be observed. In both films the male characters turn their heads to look after women, chat them up and use derogatory expressions for them. However, even these male customs seem to lose their persuasiveness and appear ridiculous in the face of the presented role changes in the films.

By and large, *Brassed Off* and *The Full Monty* stray from the traditional representations of men and women and their roles in society, whereas *Brassed Off* is still stronger bound to the traditional gender roles than *The Full Monty* is. However, both films show men as ' physically redundant in the workplace and emotionally retarded in the home' (Hallam 2000: 266).

5. *Regional Identity*

Another important signifier of the working class and a popular representation in films is the workers' attachment to place (Hill 2000a: 178). The trend to change the setting from the metropolitan environment to the "other" England of the industrial north and the Midlands in order to get a more realistic description of the working class goes back to the New Wave films of the 1950s and 1960s (Eley 1995: 19; Higson: 138). This tendency was revived in the mid-1990s, when 'film-makers in Britain [...] showed a renewed interest in portraying working class life, projecting images of alienation and crisis amidst landscapes of industrial recession and economic decline' (Hallam 2000: 261). These films are mostly set in the north of England, at locations which are well-known for their heavy industries, such as Yorkshire or the Midlands. As Hallam (2000: 266) points out, many films of the 1990s foreground a 'sense of place' in their use of location shooting and vernacular dialogue.

With regard to the films *Brassed Off* and *The Full Monty*, this 'sense of place' can clearly be made out. Both films are set in Yorkshire, a formerly highly industrialised area – *Brassed Off* in a fictional village called Grimley, *The Full Monty* in Sheffield. In both cases the local heavy industries – in *Brassed Off* the coal pit, in *The Full Monty* the steel works – determine the character and the appearance of the locality. In *The Full Monty* the decay of the Sheffield industries is particularly focused on: the characters are seen in a canal which is no longer used and in a disused and dilapidated factory hall. Typical for *The Full Monty* are, furthermore, extended panoramas over the city, or, as Higson (1996: 138) calls it: 'That Long Shot of Our Town from That Hill'. The film's characters are seen jogging, playing soccer, pondering and attempting suicide (Lomper) on a hill at the edge of the town looking down on Sheffield and its disused steel factories. In *Brassed Off* the still existing coal pit determines Grimley's character as well. It can be seen from nearly any point of the workers' residential area, it is printed on a poster in the pub and it is sewn on a flag in the brass band's rehearsal room.

Apart from the depiction of actual British industrial landscapes, the authenticity of place is, furthermore, represented through the characters' language. All working class characters in *Brassed Off* and *The Full Monty* speak the local accent, which does not only mirror their regional belonging, but also their class affiliation, since people of the lower ranks tend to speak their local accent. Furthermore, they use a lot of slang words which is another indication of their social status. In contrast to

that, all middle-class characters in the two films speak RP, the most elaborated English accent, and use only little colloquial language. Thus, the division between the classes is not only presented through the characters' housing or their clothes, as has been analysed above, but also through their language.

Conclusion

As this essay has shown, the representation of the working class in the films *Brassed Off* and *The Full Monty* includes stereotypical images, which go back to the characteristics of the "old" and traditional working class at the turn of the 20th century, and innovative images, which refer to the "new" working class as has existed since the middle of the 20th century. The stereotypical images of the lower ranks can, above all, be seen with regard to the representations of the social bonds between father and son and between the workmates. This goes along with a strong sense of fraternalism, solidarity and mutual aid which are represented in both films and which are an important hallmark of the traditional working class –identity. The relationship to women, however, turns out to be depicted in a more traditional way in *Brassed Off* than in *The Full Monty*, since in the latter film women do have a say in the men's problems, whereas the male characters in Brassed Off discuss their problems rather with their workmates than with their wives. Another stereotypical feature of the films is their representation of the characters' socio-economic situation and their properties. Most of the working class characters in the films lack money and can be distinguished from the middle-class characters by their poor housing, plain clothing, etc. Furthermore, *Brassed Off* and *The Full Monty* fall back upon stereotypical depictions of the working class by representing the workers as proud and tradition-conscious men. In *The Full Monty* Gaz and his friends are proud of their former occupation at the local steel works, in *Brassed Off* Danny is very proud of his colliery band and Phil and his workmates of the Great Miners Strike. However, both films show how these traditions slowly get lost in the face of the recent economic and social situation of the working class people. A final stereotypical feature which is used in both films is their strong 'sense of place', i.e. their setting at "original" places in the industrial north of England and the use of vernacular and colloquial language.

In contrast to these rather stereotypical representations of the working class, the topics of unemployment and of weakened male identity represent an innovative approach to the issue. Both films, but, above all, *Brassed Off*, focus upon men who have lost their jobs and upon the social and psychic effects of unemployment on them. One of these effects is the loss of the workers' male identity and a role change between men and women which goes along with it.

Concerning that, it can be concluded that both films, on the one hand, present new approaches to the topic of working class life and, thus, include recent economic and social developments in Britain into their narrative. On the other hand, both films also fall back upon stereotypical images of working class people. They, thus, follow the ' the social democratic narrative of suffering, social need, and collective good' (Eley 1995: 39), but do also act as 'a reminder of the continuing economic divisions within Britain' (Hill 2000a: 186).

Bibliography

- Cashmore, E. Ellis (1989). *United Kingdom? Class, Race and Gender since the War*. London: Unwin Hyman.
- Cooke, Lez (1996). "British Cinema". Nelmes, Jill (1996). *An Introduction to Film Studies*. London: Routledge.
- Dorey, Peter (ed.) (1999). *The Major Premiership: Politics and Policies under John Major, 1990-97*. London: Macmillan.
- Eley, Geoff (1995). "Distant Voices, Still Lives. The Family is a Dangerous Place: Memory, Gender, and the Image of the Working Class". Rosenstone, Robert A. (ed.) (1995). *Revisioning History: Film and the Construction of a New Past*. Princeton: Princeton UP.
- Green, Penny (1990). *The Enemy Without: Policing and Class Consciousness in the Miners' Strike*. Buckingham: Open UP.
- Hallam, Julia (2000). "Film, Class and National Identity: Re-Imagining Communities in the Age of Devolution". Ashby, Justine; Higson, Andrew (eds.) (2000). *British Cinema, Past and Present*. London et al.: Routledge.
- Hayward, Susan (1996). *Key Concepts in Cinema Studies*. London: Routledge.
- Haywood, Ian (1997). *Working class Fiction: From Chartism to Trainspotting*. Plymouth: Northcote House Publishers.
- Higson, Andrew (1996). "Space, Place, Spectacle: Landscape and Townscape in the 'Kitchen Sink' Film". Higson, Andrew (ed.) (1996). *Dissolving Views: Key Writings on British Cinema*. London: Cassell.
- Hill, John (2000a). "Failure and Utopianism: Representations of the Working Class in British Cinema of the 1990s". Murphy, Robert (ed.) (2000). *British Cinema of the 90s*. London: bfi.
- Hill, John (2000b). "From the New Wave to the 'Brit-Grit': Continuity and Difference in Working class Realism". Ashby, Justine; Higson, Andrew (eds.) (2000). *British Cinema, Past and Present*. London et al.: Routledge.
- Marwick, Arthur (1990). *Class: Image and Reality*. 2nd ed. London: Macmillan.
- Monk, Claire (2000). "Underbelly UK: The 1990s Underclass Film, Masculinity and the Ideologies of 'New' Britain". Ashby, Justine; Higson, Andrew (eds.) (2000). *British Cinema, Past and Present*. London et al.: Routledge.

- *Oxford English Dictionary* (1989). 2nd ed. Oxford: Clarendon Press.
- Saunders, Peter (1990). *Social Class and Stratification*. London: Routledge.
- Teske, Doris (2002). *Cultural Studies: Great Britain*. Berlin: Cornelsen.